# CONTENTS

# COLOR TEST PAGE

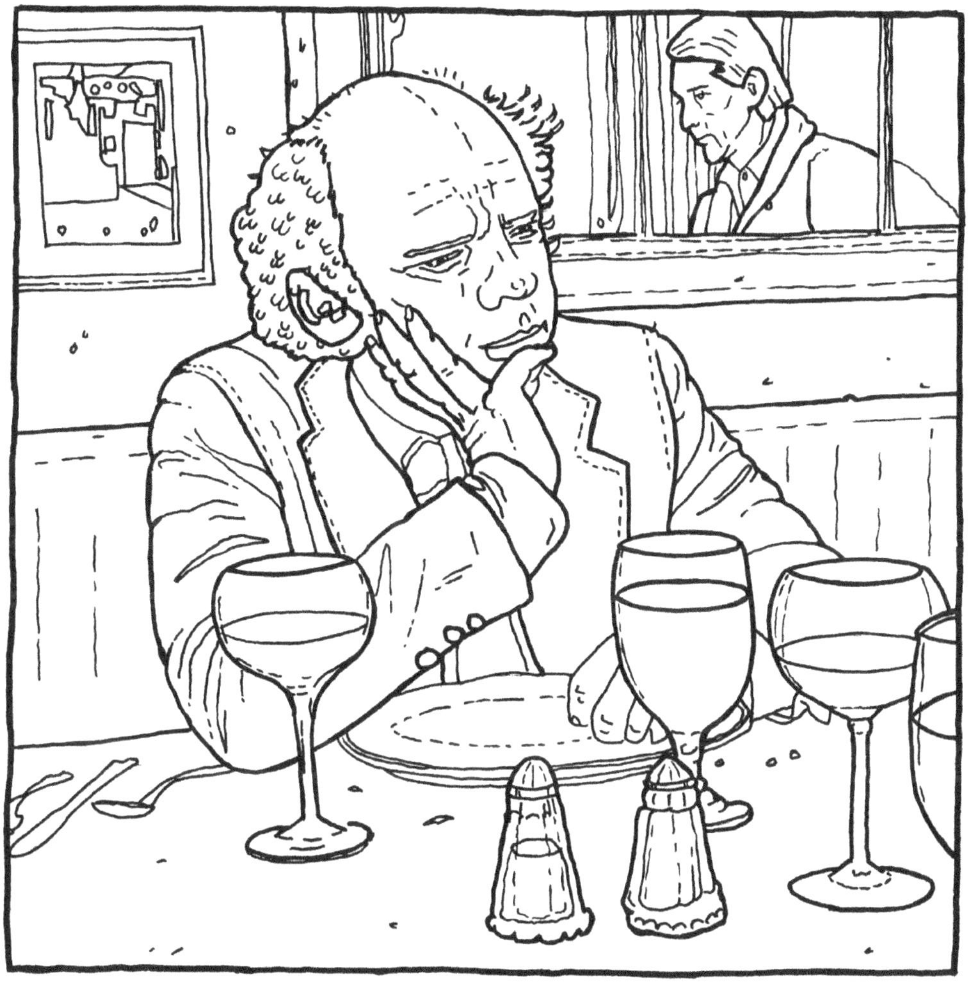

WALLACE:

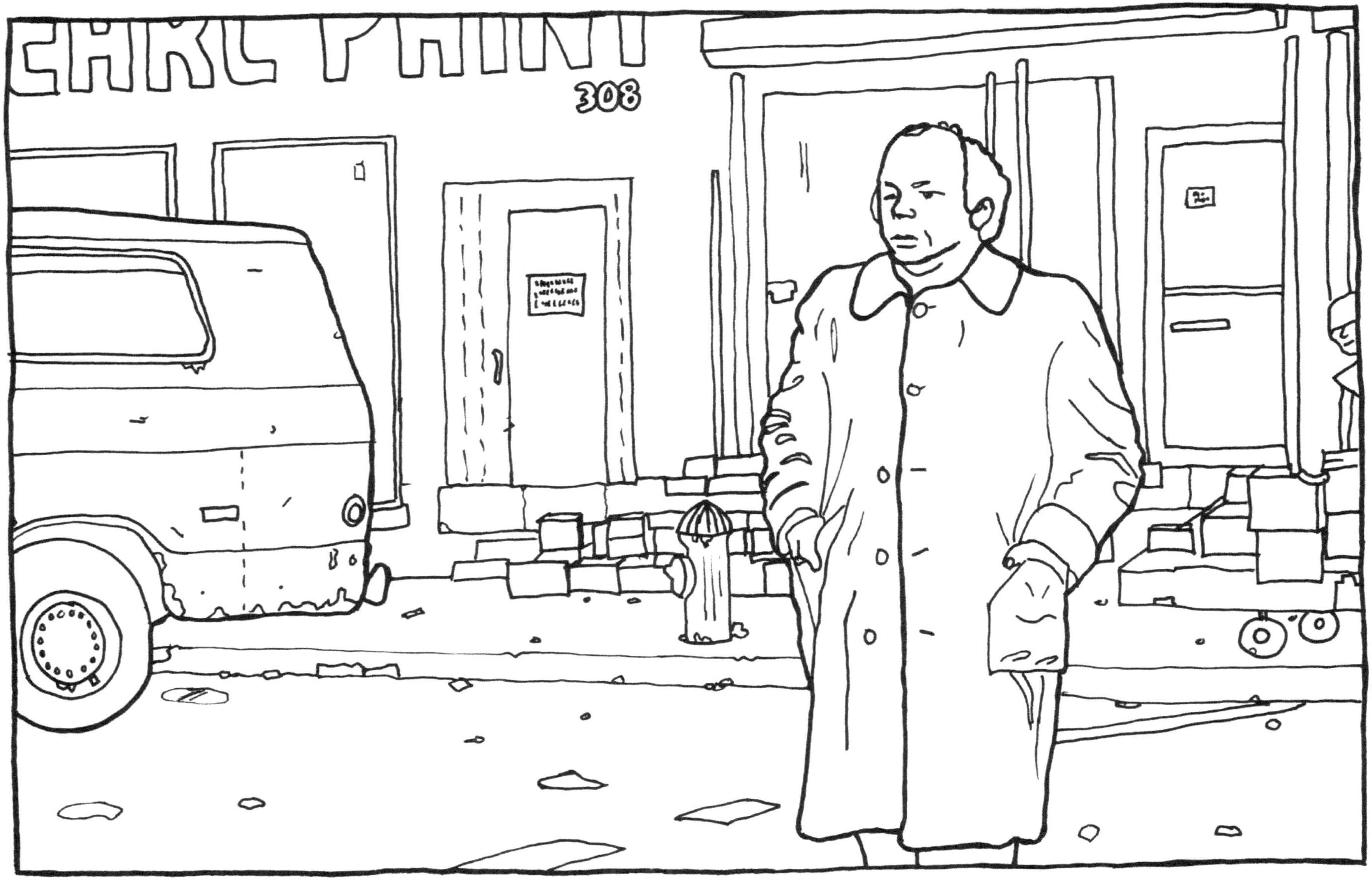
308

WALLACE:

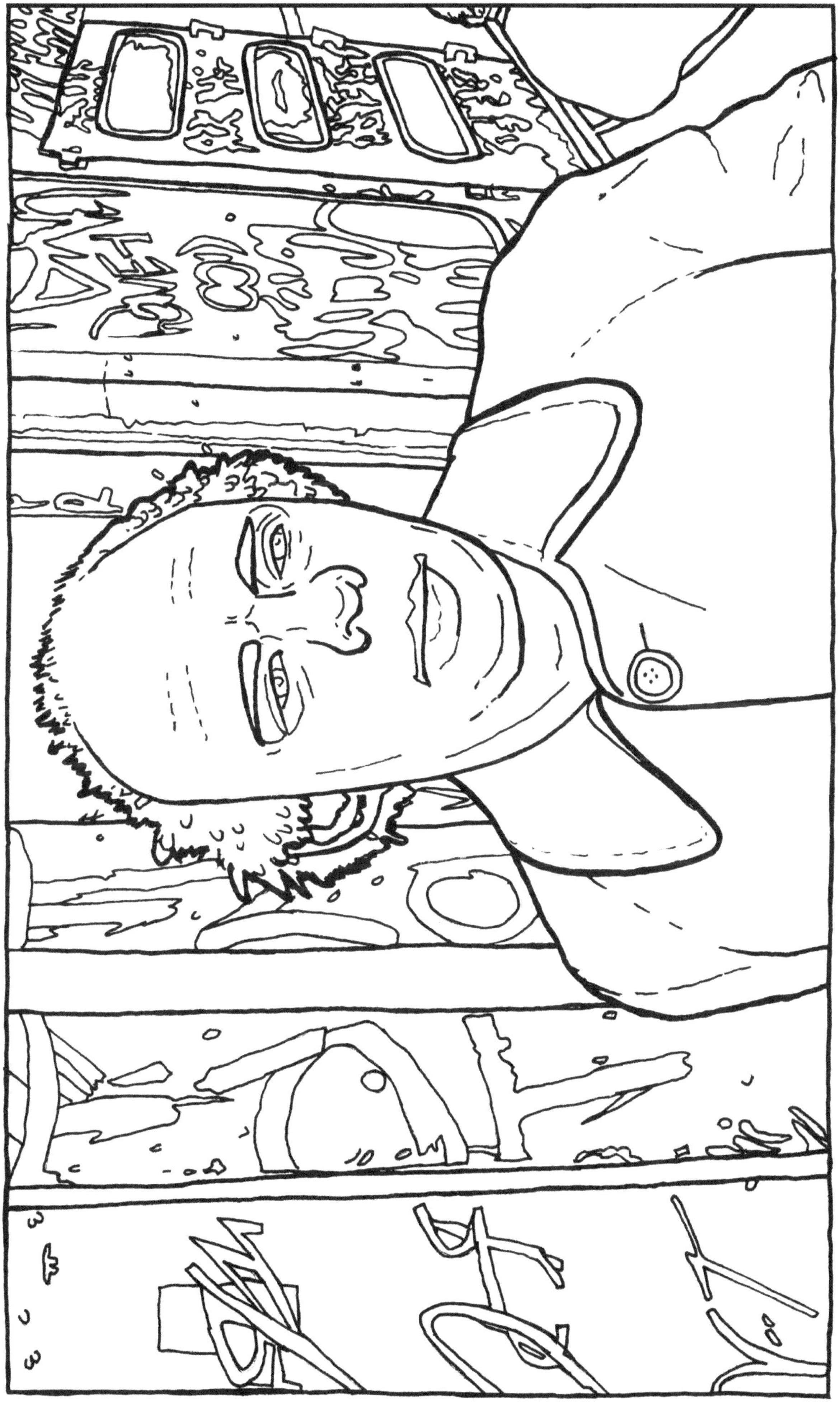

ANDRE:

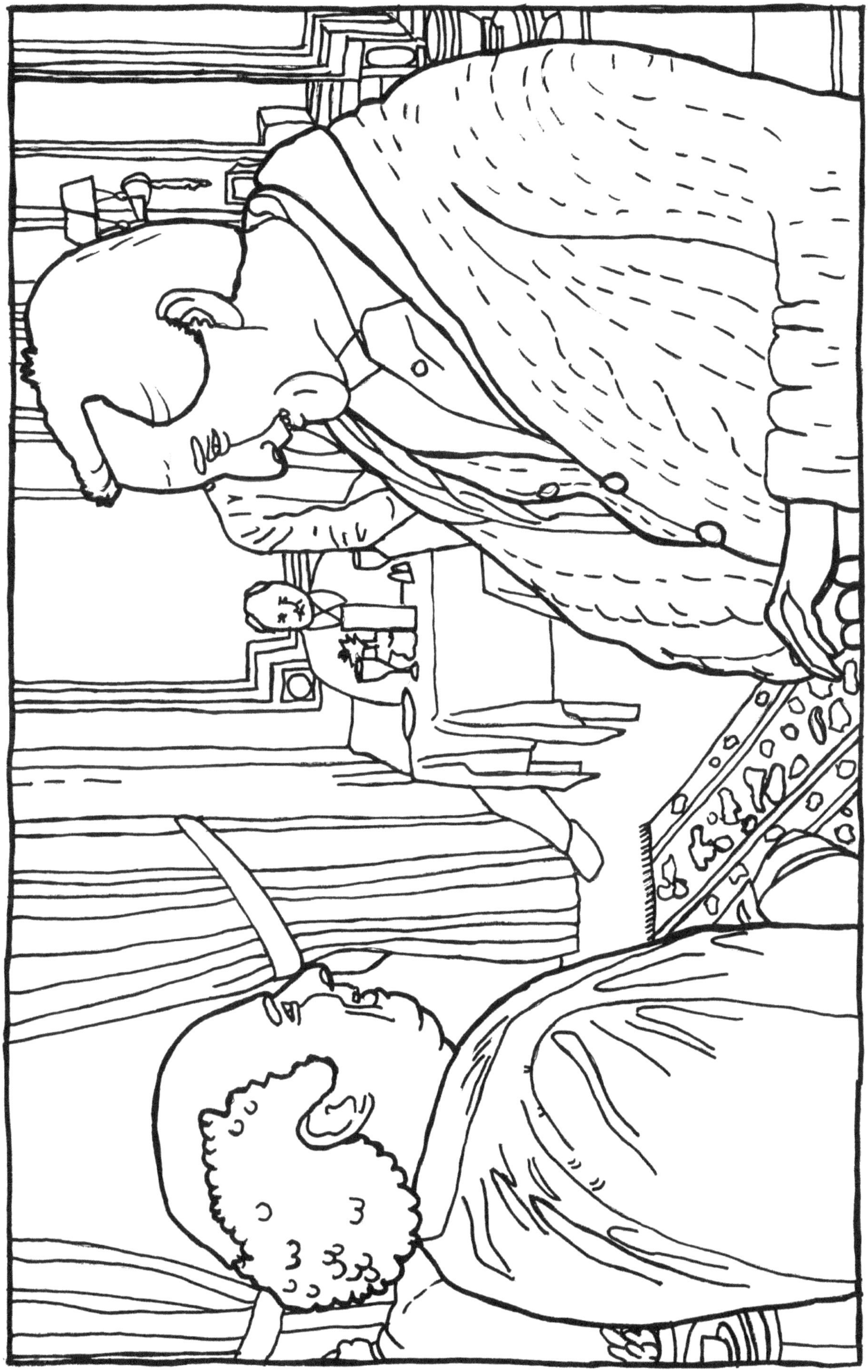

WALLACE:

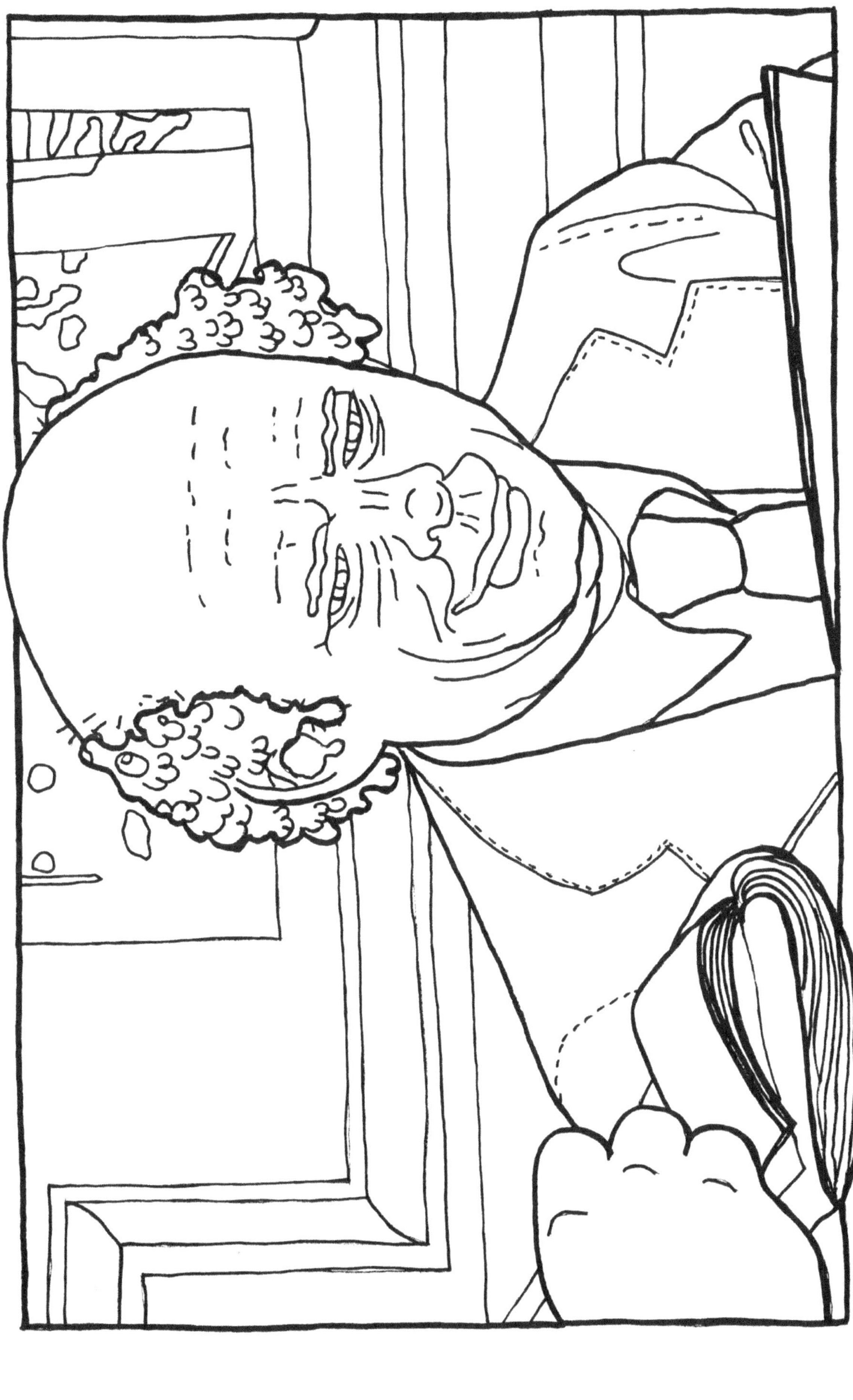

WALLACE:

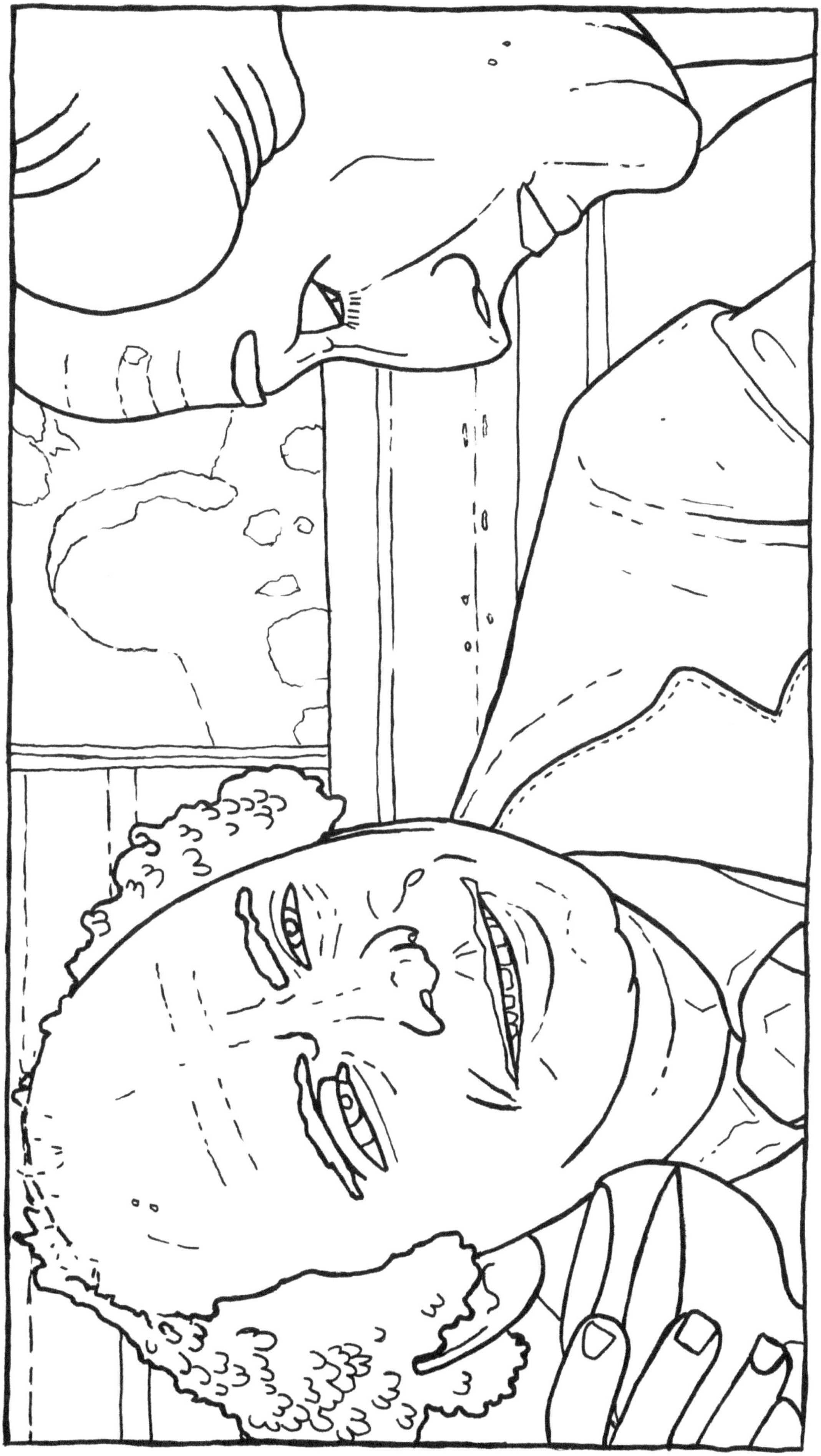

ANDRE:

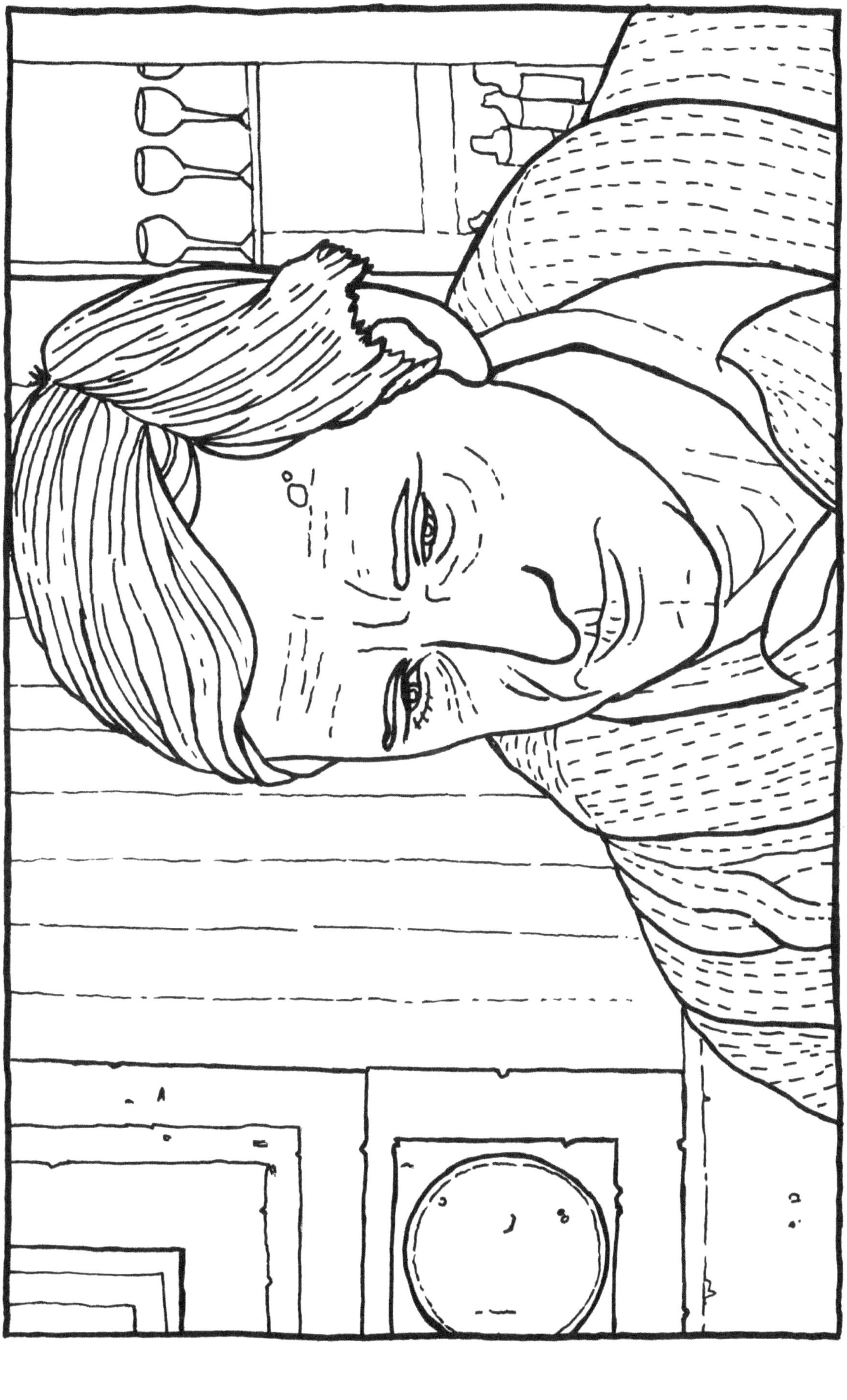

WALLACE:

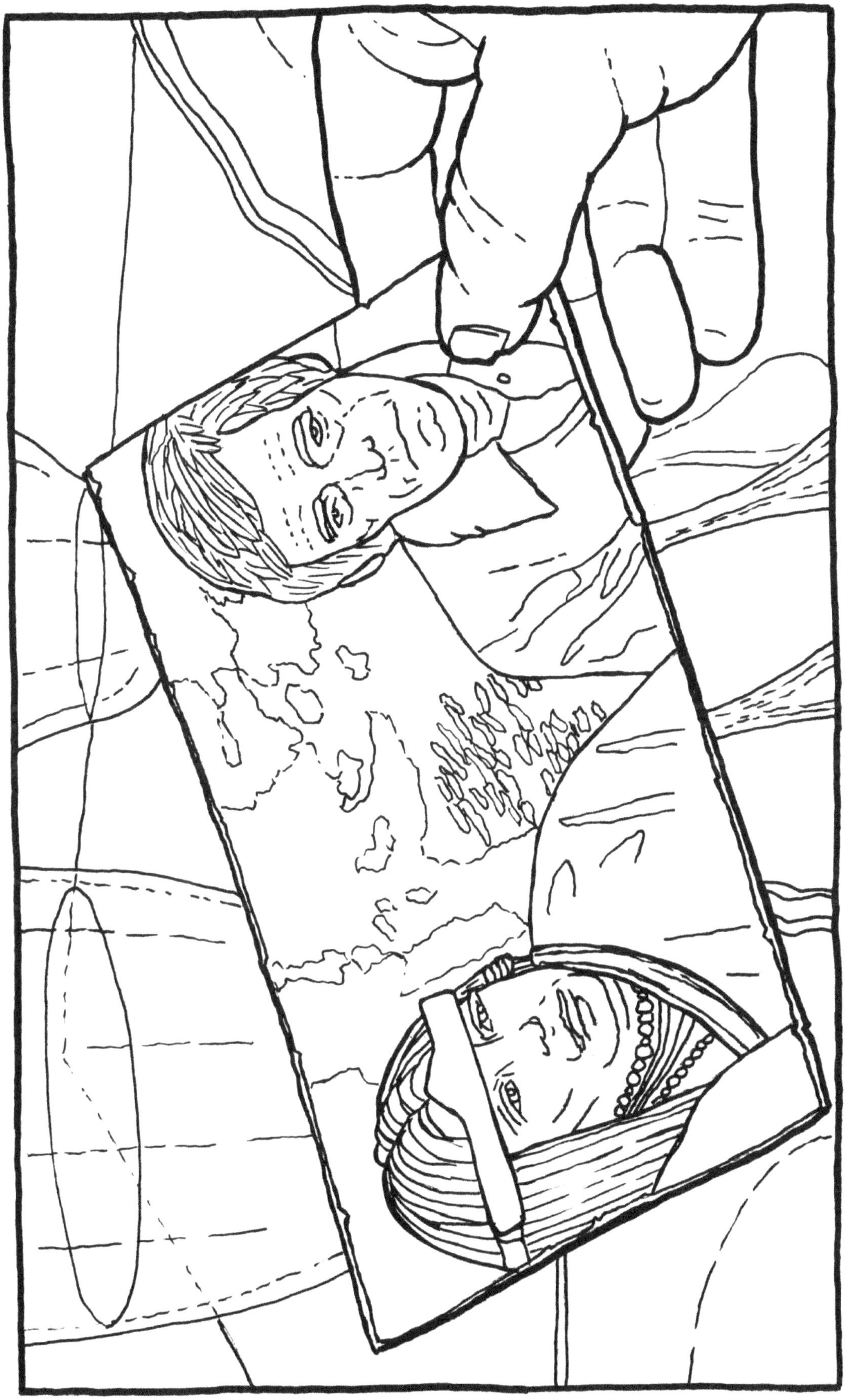

ANDRE:

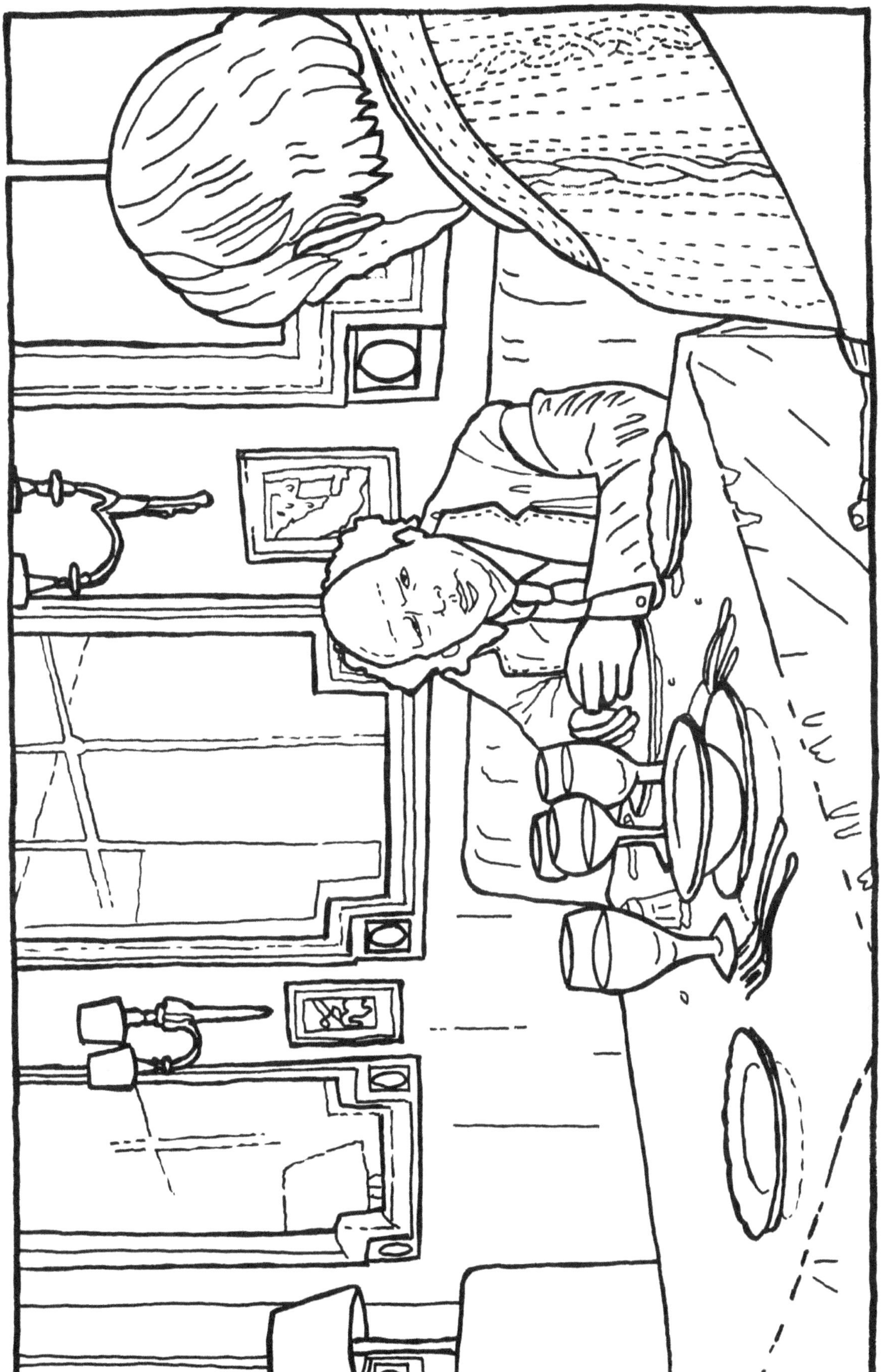

ANDRE:

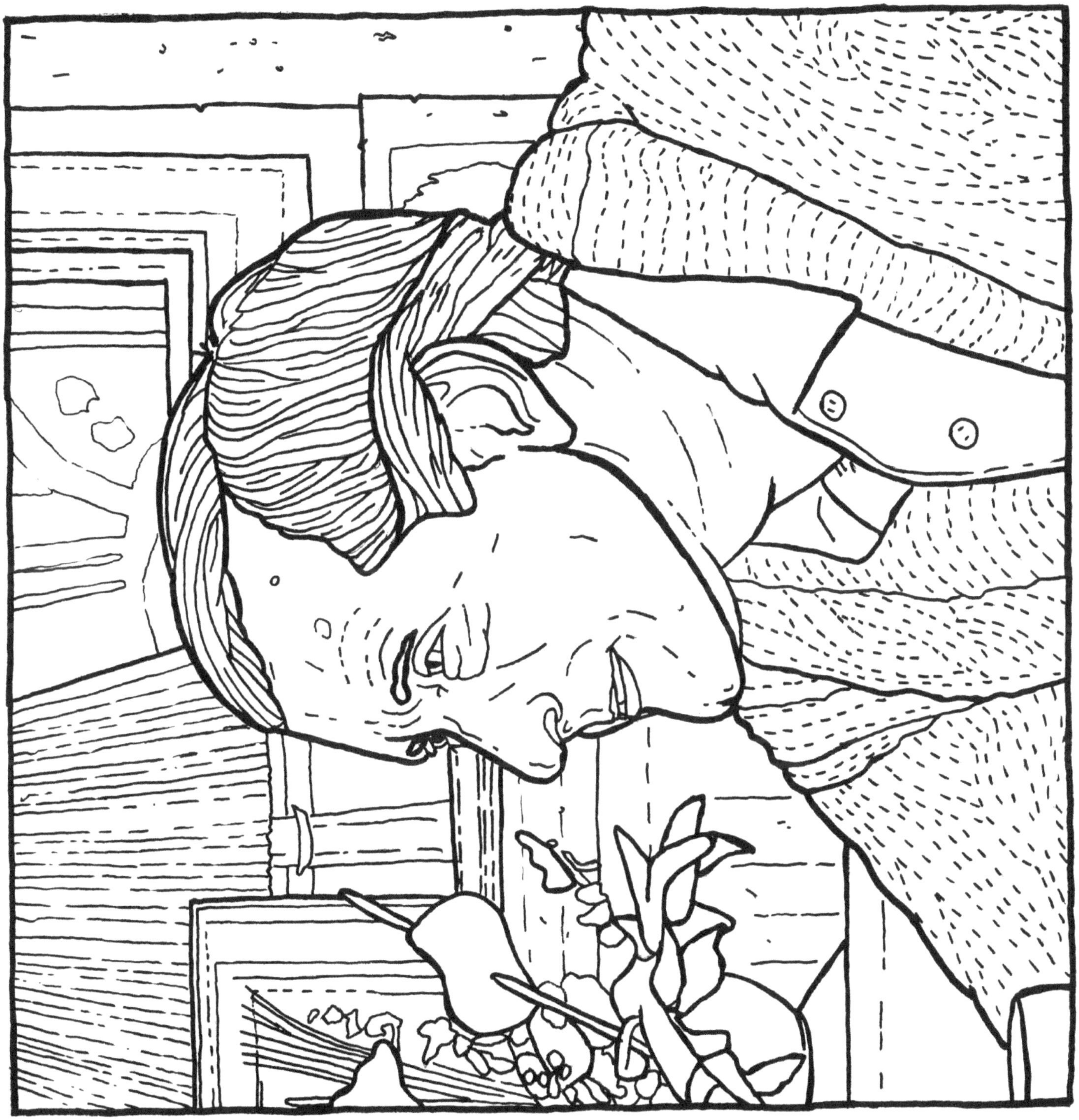

WALLACE:

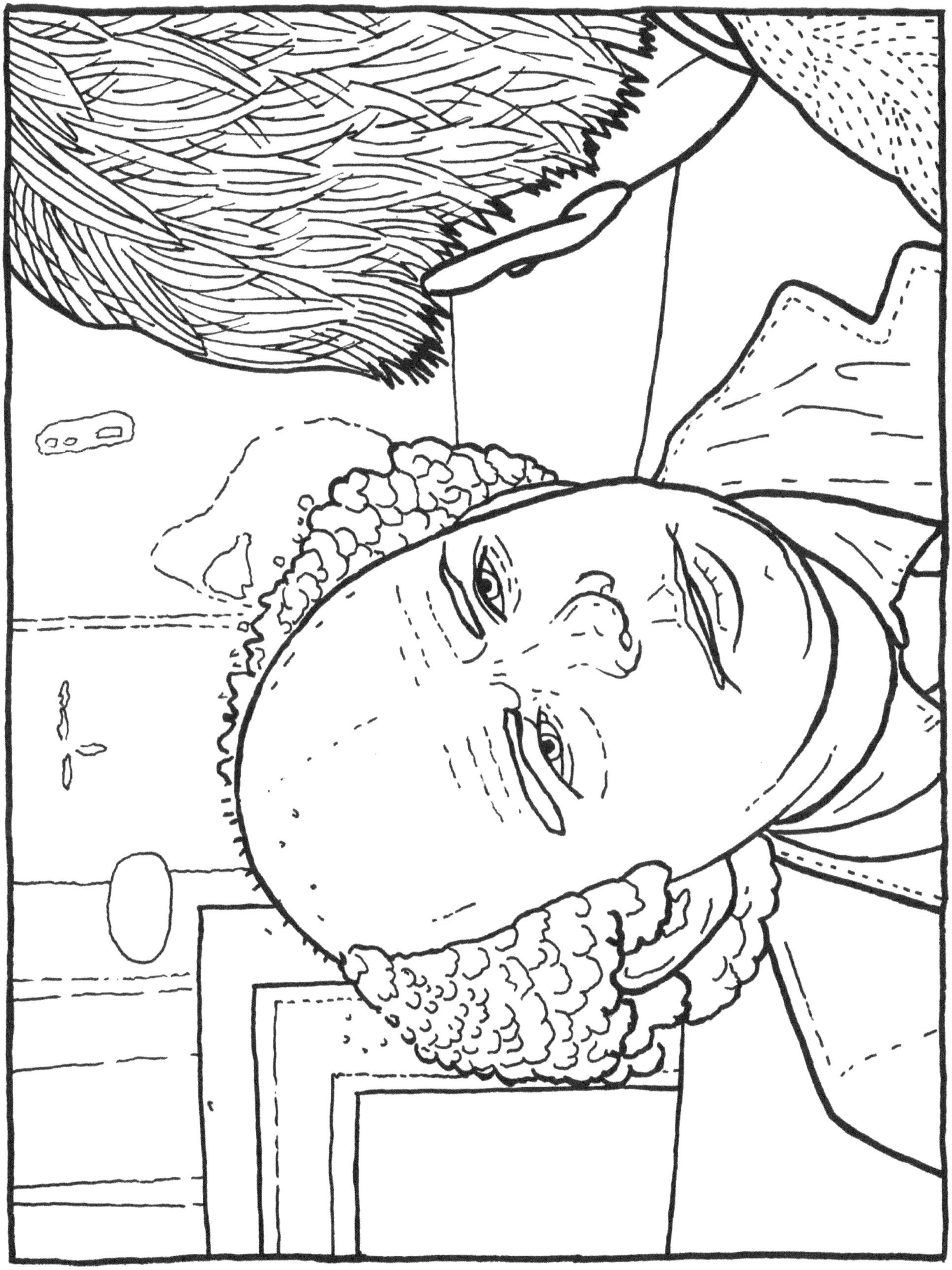

ANDRE:

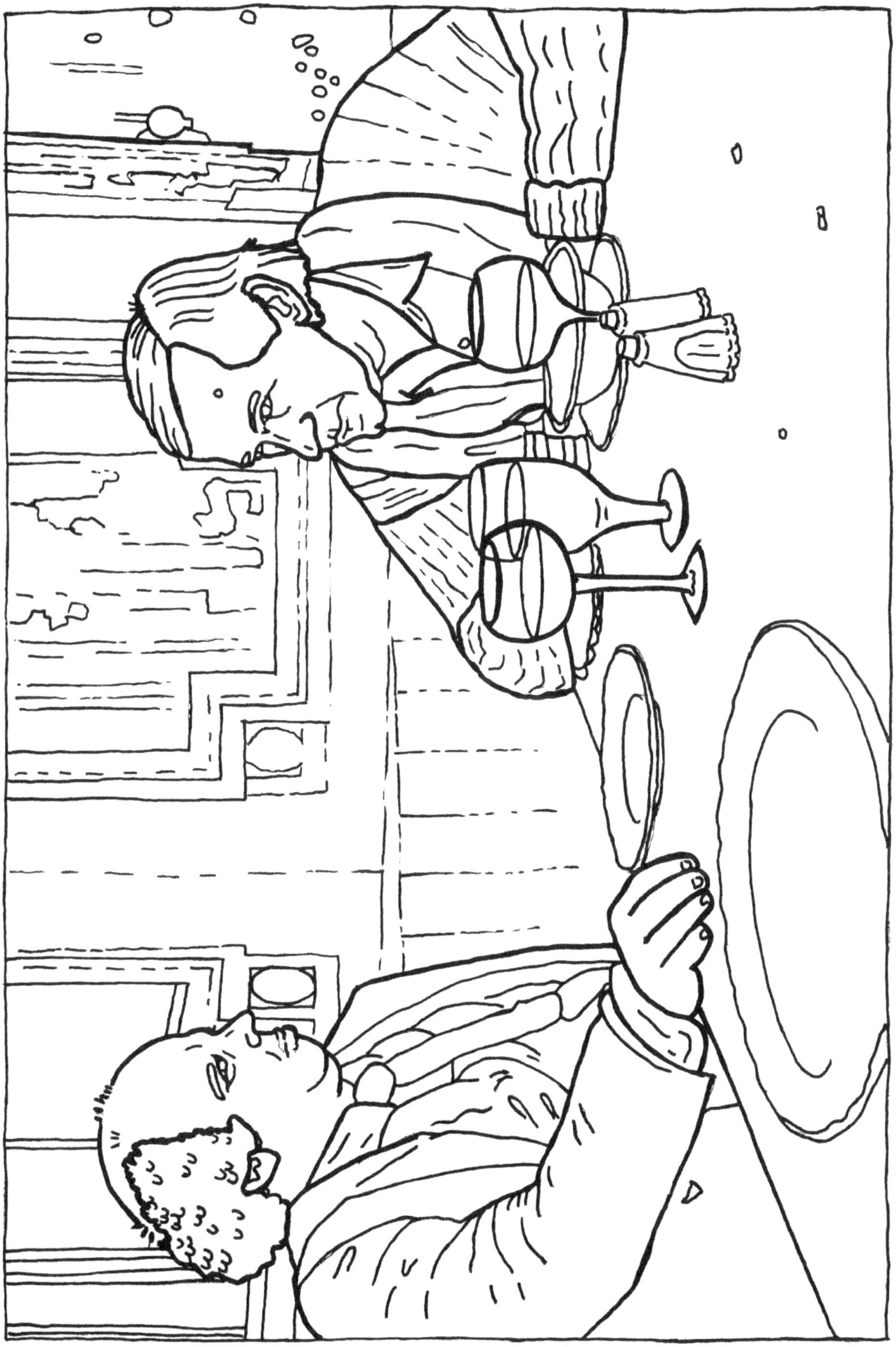

ANDRE:

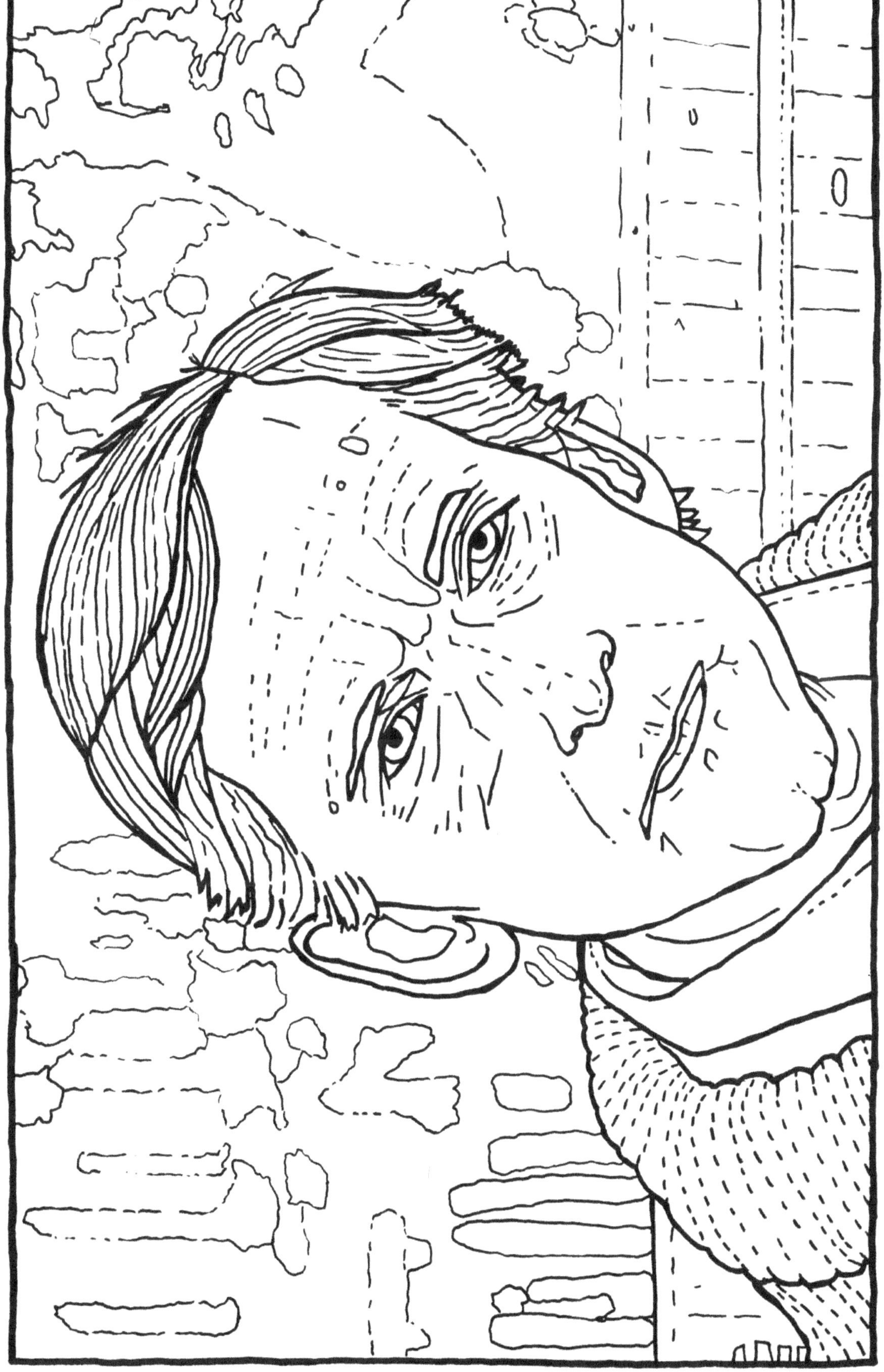

WALLACE:

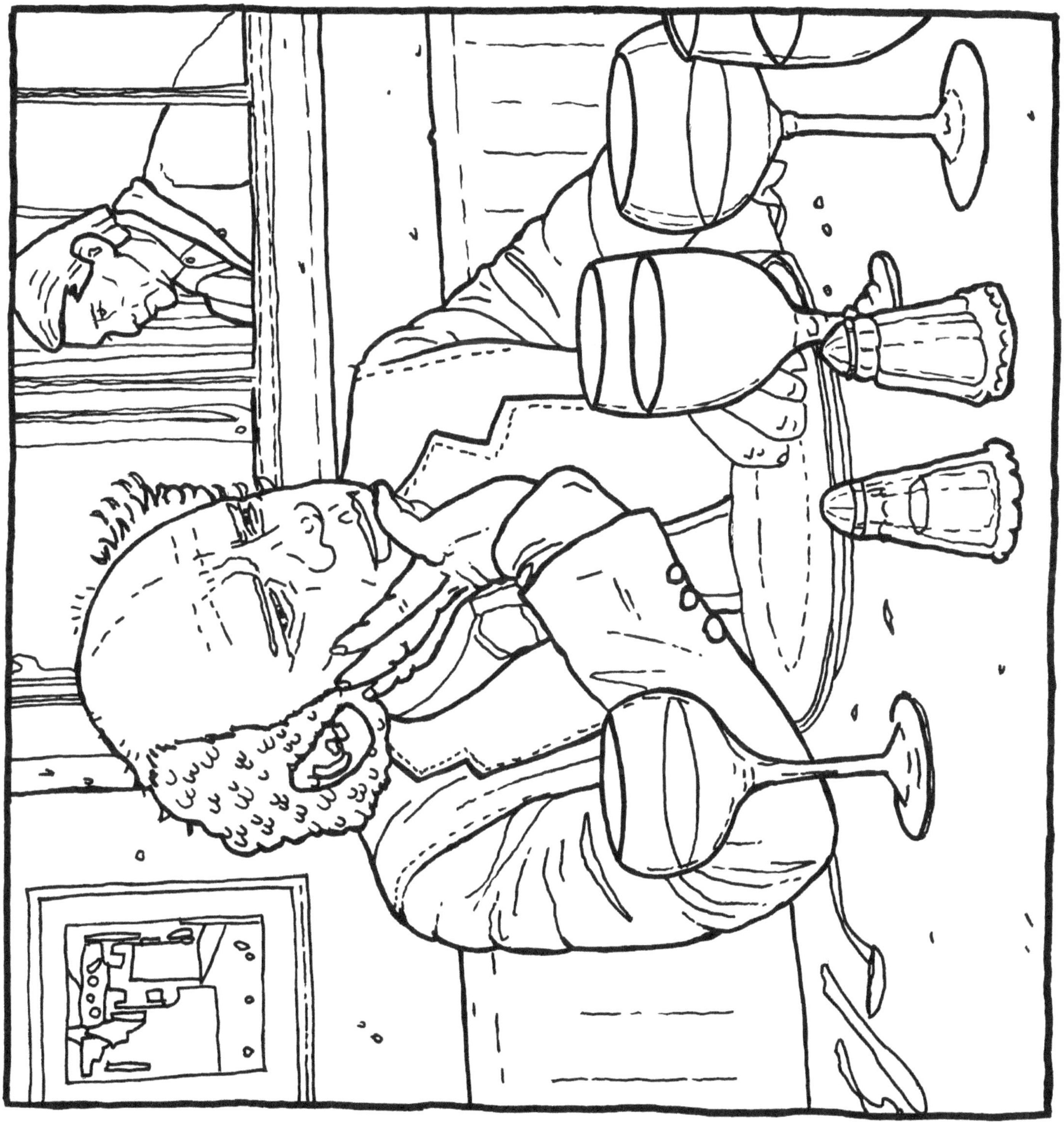

ANDRE:

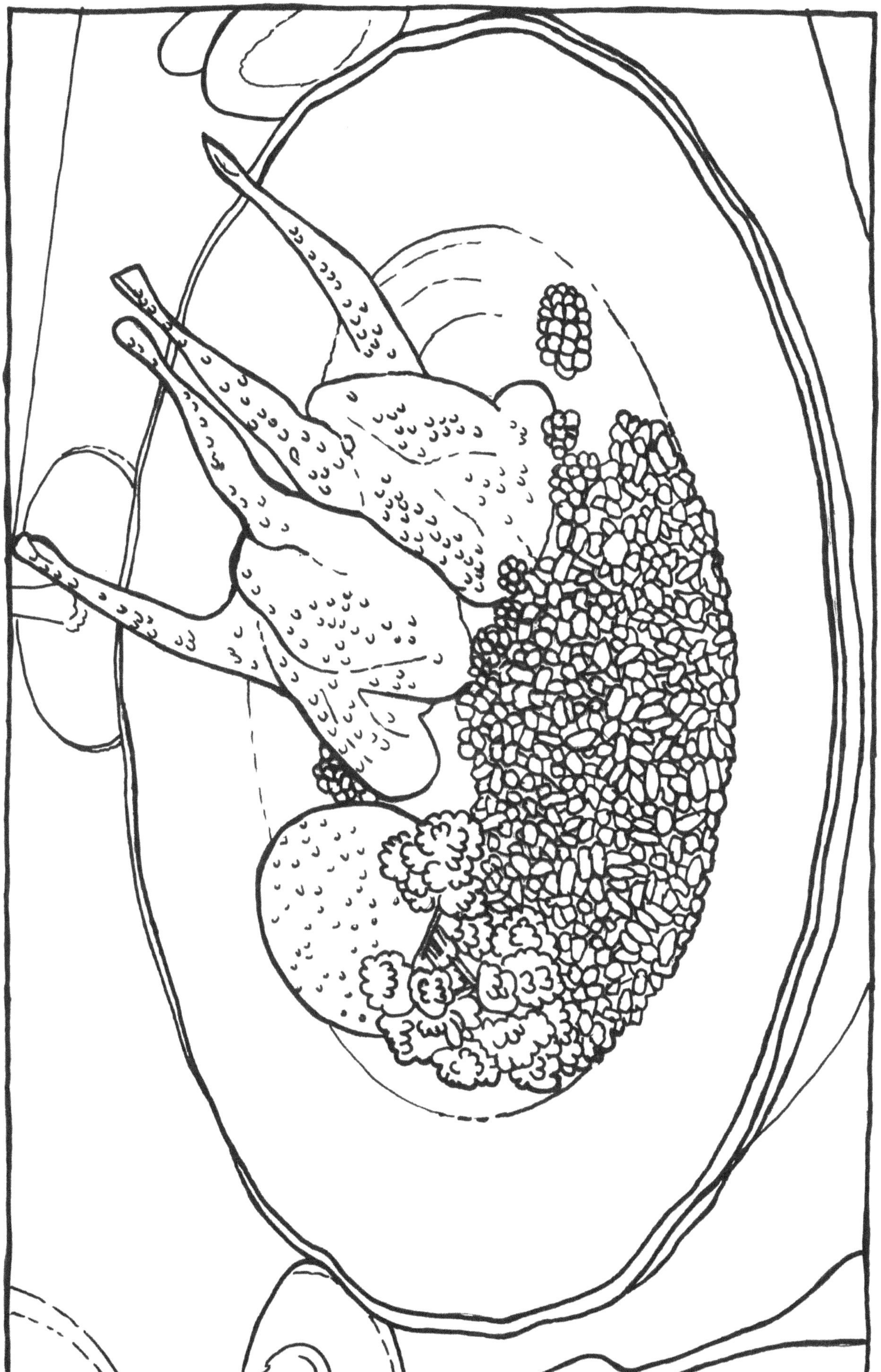

www.ingramcontent.com/pod-product-compliance
Lightning Source LLC
Chambersburg PA
CBHW081317180526
45170CB00007B/2747